Commander-in-Chief
(The 44th President)

Commander-in-Chief (The 44th President)

I merged into we, and we became one . . .

Ollie Marshall-Rico

Library of Congress Control Number:		2013908787
ISBN:	Hardcover	978-1-4836-4123-2
	Softcover	978-1-4836-4122-5
	Ebook	978-1-4836-4124-9

This book was printed in the United States of America.

Rev. date: 07/10/2013

To order additional copies of this book, contact:
Xlibris LLC
1-888-795-4274
www.Xlibris.com
Orders@Xlibris.com
131616

Contents

I. The Torch

II. The State of Campaigning

III. Workaholic

IV. The People Spoke

V. Second Term

VI. Newtown

VII. Fiscal Cliff

1

The Torch

Mr. President

Mr. President, how are you leaning, forward or backward?
Four years have yonder gone, recession was almost upon us.
The housing market was without growth.
The jobless lined miles around with eyes of sadness.

Mr. President, how are you leaning, forward or backward?
The Wall Street Market was down, looking in yonder years, hope was dim.
Four years I have been hibernating; now I am awake and back.
Just tell me the bare facts, Mr. President, nothing more or less!

Mr. President, how are you leaning, forward or backward?
Gridlock, bipartisanship, I don't want to hear about that, Mr. President!
Does the ill still stand without a hope of care to cure the pains?
Is there a sense of light for those who were struggling and
opening jobless doors?

Mr. President, how are you leaning, forward or backward?
You are the Chief, the Man, who stands above all, who has been chosen.
This country and the world stand upon your shoulders of leadership.
Mr. President, where have you taken us?

Mr. President, how are you leaning, forward or backward?
Have you equalized that work equation of those who stood below?
People were crying for a change, fear and trepidation engulfed our nation.
Recession danced upon depression when you first stepped into that office!

Mr. President, how are you leaning, forward or backward?
I want nothing but the facts, Mr. President, tell me, I have been hibernating.
Have closed closets opened up to receive all elements within this nation?
Nothing but the facts, Mr. President, I want nothing but the facts.
How are you leaning, forward or backward?

The First Family

The door opened and the surprise stood.
It was a real African-American family in the White House.
A father, a mother, two children and they were all normal.
They were not only African-Americans; they were also the First Family.
An American dream has come full circle.

His Mother

Yes, he's black, but his birth was through a powerful white mother.
She taught him well, surrounded by ideas to ravage his mind.
The image of his Kenyan father was implanted through her eyes.
Like her father, she carried the people's thoughts.

Yes, he's black, but his birth was through a powerful white mother.
She distanced him from his birthplace; they traveled to Indonesia.
At the appropriate time, she returned him to her father, his grandfather.
It was there in that environment he continued to emulate his father's ideas.

Yes, he's black, but his birth was through a powerful white mother.
Father's ghost, ghost or not, he emulates "total America".
He represents the total evil of this country with its goodness.
It is through him, everything is blended into one whole of greatness.

Yes, he's black, but his birth was through a powerful white mother.
The gifted genius of his father lies within his walls of ideas.
Through his mother, his father's ideas are rooted.
His mother's family is the new Underground Railroad, the people's choice.

Yes, he's black, but his birth was through a powerful white mother.
He has accomplished all that America represents.
Ideas are plenty; he represents the best of America.
Hope is now where there was none.

The Lady from Kansas

She gave birth to a president, President Obama.
Kansas was her birthplace.
He claimed victory not in Kansas.
There the streets still hold her family line.

She gave birth to a president, President Obama.
She developed love through another country line.
They met and embraced through a third continent.
With others, Africa, Europe, and North America entailed one classroom.

She gave birth to a president, President Obama.
He served her well.
Her bell has long tolled.
Medical insurance escaped her,
but he erased a duplicated suffering with a bill.

She gave birth to a president, President Obama.
Unfortunate people were the lives she sought to serve.
She was always true to her character;
she served actively those who were in need.
This birth child carries her genes to serve not only the unfortunate but all.

Indonesia

He has his mother's heart that beats for all.
Indonesia came with eyes to see.
Not a paw of cleanness, it was a raw environment.
The rich had all, and the poor had not a wall.

He has his mother's heart that beats for all.
Indonesia's exotic environment captivated the young boy's eyes.
Deep within himself, in the mist of poverty, he began the hunt for self.
Who am I and where do I belong?

He has his mother's heart that beats for all.
In a distant country, a quest for self began to evolve.
This enchanted journey was one of two that launched him into his future.
He was compelled to question the level of poverty worldwide.

He has his mother's heart that beats for all.
At this young age, perhaps his mother viewed restlessness in her son.
From Indonesia to Hawaii he went, in the care of her parents.
They wrapped him in the love of a dove, and that is the love he knew.

Kenyan Blood

The land of my father, Kenya, was deep in my blood.
I was shaped by his path.
I have carried my father's path into the future as no other.
His absent image has always been strong in my mind.

The land of my father, Kenya, was deep in my blood.
I would follow his path; I had not a choice—my mother ruled.
He, my father, was an honorable man.
An honorable man was he; that I would be too.

The land of my father, Kenya, was deep in my blood.
The land I would claim one day, my feet would touch its soil.
It would be the same soil that had once touched my father's toes.
It was like birth all over again, the day my feet touched Kenya's soil.

The land of my father, Kenya, was deep in my blood.
My circle completed, weight was lifted from my life; Kenya's soil spoke.
My life has become an obligation to others;
intellectualism has to denote active responsibility to serve others.
Theory had to be a reality, a people's reality to move forward justly.

Kenya—The Man

His brilliance lies within the President.
The gifted orator speaks, and the crowd roars with approval.
It is the strength of his father that is compelling.
Abandoned, yes, but vision of his father echoed throughout his lifestyle.

His brilliance lies within the President.
He traveled many roads, from Africa to America.
He touched the lives of many, none greater than his son, Barack.
There, he left the stroke of a President.

His brilliance lies within the President.
Rooted in Kenya's culture, he enriched others with his cultural lifestyle.
A young bride he took; through them, they created President Barack Obama.
A President who emerged, not on color of one people, but on character.

His brilliance lies within the President.
He lies deep within Kenya's soil.
He speaks, "Barack, you have achieved an almost unachieveable goal."
The voice from the grave speaks.

The Torch

His father gave him an image to grow into a whole person.
He dreamed the smell of his father that carried his roots.
He carried the words of his father through his mother's eyes.
The road to Kenya helped open, connect and bridge him into a whole.

His father gave him an image to grow into a whole person.
His father's lifestyle echoed from his mother,
a man of high character she visualized.
His father's pain became his struggle, and they both merged into one.
It is through this that he became motivated to become President Obama.

His father gave him an image to grow into a whole person.
The conflict lies between the haves and the have-nots.
His father's honor is carried through his bloodline.
His father's genes run heavily through his bones.

His father gave him an image to grow into a whole person.
Idealism comes with a great hope for the future.
It is a mark of a dream that shines with hope.
He aligned himself with his father, although there was distance.

His father gave him an image to grow into a whole person.
His mother, grandparents, and role models paved that connected road.
His father cut corners not.
Kenya travel awakened him to go forth with the torch.

Conflict

Conflict comes and conflict goes.
It is through life's conflict we are always in search of self.
Loved ones sometime bring conflict out of deep affection.
It is the ghost that sometimes searches for a deeper meaning in oneself.

Conflict comes and conflict goes.
We reach for truth in search of self.
It is through the love and conflict with others we sometime find ourselves.
The road is never pudding smooth in finding the inner being of self.

Conflict comes and conflict goes.
One may find himself adored and loved by most
if comfortable in his own skin.
It is the embodiment of self-awareness that will bring change in oneself.
He who is comfortable with himself will bring comfort to others.

Conflict comes and conflict goes.
One should not allow another to define one's being.
It is through change and hope we come to believe in tomorrow.
We reach a height of inner being when we overcome our differences.

Separation

It was a separation that cried out for a reconnection.
Trinity Church had given the President a community connection.
He found a place to claim with a spiritual purpose.
He connected strongly with the people, and they shielded their son.

It was a separation that cried out for a reconnection.
The community cried when he and the pastor separated ways.
They prayed silently for the end to come and a reconnected bond.
When it became impossible, many wanted the pastor to just shut up.

It was a separation that cried out for a reconnection.
Trinity Church is a strong bond in the community with its political ties.
It was the church that married him and the First Lady and
baptized their children.
It was like a marriage separation; the bond had been broken, we cried.

It was a separation that cried out for a reconnection.
The glass was not cracked; it had been broken, and we had to move forward.
Family members took sides, most took the side of the President;
we accepted closure.
The country wanted and needed to move forward.

It was a separation that cried out for a reconnection.
We dismissed everything that hindered the country from moving forward.
The President has always stayed on the upbeat.
He rode into the office not once but twice on the heart of the people.

Sandy Hook

Each family lost has been infectious throughout the nation.
Tears have ripped out walls.
Stone shock was on broken faces.
The atmosphere was full of sadness.

Each family lost has been infectious throughout the nation.
Tragedy has grabbed these families with sadness unthinkable.
Yes, hearts are broken and tears are flowing.
This is a cycle that calls out not to be repeated.

Each family lost has been infectious throughout the nation.
Sandy Hook was one merciless slaughter.
The beautiful laughter in little voices, they are gone forever.
The element of time cannot be clocked back;
we live with yesterday's tragedy.

Each family lost has been infectious throughout the nation.
The tearful President's eyes speak for all who are trying to cope.
There is not a left or right here with the President,
just flowing shared tears . . .
Drowning tears, tears that have drown before they actually leave the eyes.

Each family lost has been infectious throughout the nation.
Twenty innocent bodies lay in the morgue, plus six who sought to protect.
Children who walked innocently one moment,
their lives were stolen less than a flash of a second.
Answers we must grip, bury selfishness; our future lies within the children.

II

The State of Campaigning

A Voice of Change

The early day came and went, and you have hung tough.
Many people believed it wouldn't or couldn't happen, but you held tough.
First there were few in numbers with constant exhaustion;
yes, but enthusiasm gaps existed not.
Money was little to none, but the belief was strong.

The early day came and went, and you have hung tough.
They loved their country; they believed and
they wanted it changed to represent all.
They had strong hope, bare walls, homemade signs, and little steak to eat.
They came on all levels, colors, ages, and with the slogan "Yes, we can."

The early day came and went, and you have hung tough.
With determined spirit, they illustrated one nation, one people.
They wanted a man who would speak their voice, and you had been chosen.
They no longer wanted an outdated policy that spoke not their interest.

The early day came and went, and you have hung tough.
Through you, everyone had a chance to achieve the American Dream.
They wanted you to be their champion in Washington to carry their voice.
A voice of change to bring forth or to stop the current policy—it would
be their voice.

Code Words

The code word **race** is still calling with many voices.
Were they brazen enough to call the President lazy!
What, dumb is the price on Rice's head, a Rhodes Scholar!
When will it stop, now or never?

The code word **race** is still calling with many voices.
White is right; black, step back.
She had hardly a second grade geography knowledge.
They put her in a position to step into a President's shoes.

The code word **race** is still calling with many voices.
What thick trick are they trying to conjure up now?
Voter oppression, it became a pull-out-vote campaign.
The youth and old were strutting in pairs to cast their votes.

The code word **race** is still calling with many voices.
They created untruths at your footsteps and tried to mislead others
with colored coded words.
Not coping, are you for real? You yelled succession—this is and
shall remain one nation!
You live in a blind trust, free of progressiveness, encroached with racism.

The code word **race** is still calling with many voices.
Color me colorless beyond my skin.
We bleed, we hurt, we cry.
We speak the truth, not by color but honor.

Racism

A world free of racism may never exist.
But people who choose to make a difference can develop a new road map.
People coming together as one can magnify one mass change.
It can be a force to overcome those who wish to
destroy one's political power.

A world free of racism may never exist.
It may be annihilated with those who choose to speak with open voices.
It is a world that can be shocked into reality.
But, it cannot be removed from lips for those who choose not to change.

A world free of racism may never exist.
Safe, customized ways often refuse to ever alter into new ones.
They live, they breathe, and they expect others to adapt to their standards.
A world tied into their ancient family rituals.

A world free of racism may never exist.
When new birth comes perhaps old ways will slowly die.
But it still comes with deadly weapons to mingle among the masses.
A world may never entirely be free of racism.

Changing Times

Change your policy; you will fare a better chance the next time.
Curve your racism, a large number of whites voted for President Obama.
Speak to the needs of the community; it may respond to you.
It's not about color; it's how the country defines its need.

Change your policy; you will fare a better chance the next time.
What sane mother will vote against her daughter's interests?
Open your door to receive today's news.
Women are walking the roads independently.

Change your policy; you will fare a better chance the next time.
What sane father will vote against his son's interests?
A young man seeks hopefully to capture an independent woman by his side.
It is a combining force to move swiftly forward.

Change your policy; you will fare a better chance the next time.
Rooted racism is a dying force.
Walk with the changing time to bridge the new gap.
There are olive branches all around you, grip on to one to swing in time.

The First of the First

It was an unforgettable, historical time.
The first African American president had been elected.
Two worlds exist in this country, one racist and one nonracist.
Youth, blacks, Hispanics, women, and white males put him in office.

It was an unforgettable, historical time.
Many did not believe that it would happen, both black and white.
They felt the elements of this country would not allow it.
The John Birch Society, KKK, and the Skinheads were too deeply rooted.

It was an unforgettable, historical time.
Many blacks were in self-doubt, to conceive this, was beyond their minds.
Yet there were other blacks who finally made the transition.
Women stood firmly with their belief, and men echoed forward, finally.

It was an unforgettable, historical time.
Reality shocked the unbelievers on the first Tuesday of November 2008.
A black man had finally been elected, the President of the USA.
The racists from the House echoed, "We will make sure he will serve only once."

It was an unforgettable, historical time.
Serve two, he may not; but he has already made an impact.
The Obama Health Care has been instituted.
Many former Presidents—Nixon, Regan and Clinton—were unsuccessful
with this mode.

It was an unforgettable, historical time.
The Detroit Automobile Company was going belly-up; he saved it.
The country was on the verge of depression; he pulled it out.
Yes, he may not serve two terms; but an impact he has already made.

The Last Hurrah

He came; they had gathered with signs, with words of encouragement.
He shared his stories, beginning to the end, at his last hurrah.
He traced his path to this point at his last hurrah.
His eyes were teary at his last hurrah.

He came; they had gathered with signs, with words of encouragement.
He championed the end of an Iraq War at his last hurrah.
The initiator of 911, under him, he breathes no more at his last hurrah.
General Motors collapsed not; today it stands strong at his last hurrah.

He came; they had gathered with signs, with words of encouragement.
The Military became nondiscriminatory, dishonorable discharge lingers not.
Two of three ladies have championed the Supreme Court; he moves forward.
Win or lose, this is his last hurrah, his last hurrah, his last hurrah.

He came; they had gathered with signs, with words of encouragement.
Challenges were met with determined spirit at his last hurrah.
Poverty still lingers in our midst, doors need to open for those who pave
streets daily, seeking jobs, at his last hurrah.
A champion is needed to fight for the middle class at his last hurrah.

He came; they had gathered with signs, with words of encouragement.
People, who loved this country, have worked to change it through him.
The young, the old, white, black, and Native Americans have spoken.
The goal is to move forward, to continue the current policy, not backward.
At his last hurrah, sadness rings with us,
at his last hurrah, at his last hurrah.

If

The word **if** has become that raging, dangling monster.
It's the move he didn't take—if this, if that—that may cost
him this election.
The Supreme Court appointments should have been emphasized.
He brought forth Equal Pay Act for Women, if only he emphasized it.

The word **if** has become that raging, dangling monster.
If he hadn't slept through his first debate,
If I hear this word again, it will be wartime!
Especially, **if** he loses this election, this very day,
my war hat just may come off.

The word **if** has become that raging, dangling monster.
Just pray about the policies that will come forth if he is not reelected.
He has been one great president,
if not the greatest that has held that office.
At least in my time, many have walked in those shoes.

The word **if** has become that raging, dangling monster.
From Truman, thereafter, many sought to implement an act
on health as the Obamacare.
This became a reality under his domain due to his leadership.
Forget the **if,** if he's not reelected, think about his achievements.

The Wait

I have waited, waited, and waited; now this day has finally arrived!
I jumped out of bed without doing my personal!
I ran to my car and sped to the poll; off to vote I went.
Here I am; the poll is closed!

I have waited, waited, and waited; now this day has finally arrived.
A distant SUV was sitting in the parking lot.
The city clerk arrived to post a new voting location at this late hour!
Two women, approached this regular voting location, walking.

I have waited, waited, and waited; now this day has finally arrived.
I spoke sharply to the city clerk; he said, "Notification was on the Internet."
With a questionable expression, I replied "There is a power outage in this
city! Internet, what world have you been living in?"
On a lighter note, we laughed; he assured me someone would be
physically posted at this location throughout the voting hours.

I have waited, waited, and waited; now this day has finally arrived!
I collected the walkers, and we proceeded to the new voting location.
We completed voting after approximately thirty minutes.
The hours began slowly to tick away as I waited for the final results,
minus a few calls to encourage others to go vote.

I have waited, waited, and waited; now this day has finally arrived!
Will the results be near or far in the distance?
Will morning come with bodies sitting, anxiously waiting?
Will the results come this day, or will it be a bridge into the unknown?

The Organizer

The Organizer, to Chicago he went.
The foot soldier, he walked and he talked.
He sought to organize the poorest neighborhoods.
It was about teaching people to help themselves become independent.

The Organizer, to Chicago he went.
The boarded-up houses swung wide.
The corner owners had their ground.
It was about establishing a goal of hope to those who had little.

The Organizer, to Chicago he went.
It was about taking ownership to teach one or more.
The street was strong, but the will was stronger.
It was an implemented educational tool that carried the will of both parents.

The Organizer, to Chicago he went.
The neighborhood elders saw this young man working hard for the people.
He became a shining star of the neighborhood, the people's son.
They embraced him with love because he had found love within himself.

The Vessel

You are the vessel of your body.
You move with ownership, not for anyone to take or steal.
You may carry it well or carry it poorly.
That decision lies within you, so let your thoughts come through you.

You are the vessel of your body.
It is not a trash bag or can for others to dump in their discarded mess.
Leave others behind who seek to box you in like a fox boxed into a corner.
Those who represent Fox News let them swing high and low without you.

You are the vessel of your body.
Treat it well, do not allow anyone to violate it.
Let them see you standing tall as they proceed through the hall.
It is your spirit of life that should not be caged.

You are the vessel of your body.
Walk with the strength that embodies you.
Talk without pausing to those who wish to hinder your steps.
You are truly the vessel of your body.

Edith Childs

Edith had a voice stronger than a lion.
She wore her church hat without an apology.
She strolled down the road with a voice that traveled worldwide.
She labored endlessly with the phrase "**Fired Up! Ready To Go!**"

Edith had a voice stronger than a lion.
She wore her church hat without an apology.
She bounced up and down the streets as she pounded on doors.
She was always on the run, many her meals came from a hot soup pot.

Edith had a voice stronger than a lion.
She wore her church hat without an apology.
She generated energy where there was none.
There were no floors or roads too hot for her shoes.

Edith had a voice stronger than a lion.
She wore her church hat without an apology.
Edith spoke loud and clear, "Fired Up! Ready To Go!"
It was only through the uniqueness of our president that he was able to
connect the smallest community with the largest one.

"Fired Up! Ready To Go!" are energizing words.
Motivating words, words that will force the feet forward to meet another.
You kick forcefully, out of bed without a stick.
They are words that scream, "Yes, I Can! Yes, I Can!"

Pathway

Our ancestors have created a pathway for us to follow this day.
We occupy the highest office that can be obtained in this country.
We occupy with color but own not the office; no race can own that office.
It is an office that represents every color and creed within this country.

Our ancestors have created a pathway for us to follow this day.
The president is an African-American, but he represents everyone.
Related I am, but fearful many of us will not walk in that path created.
It's a path, where many have died to bring us to this new appointed day.

Our ancestors have created a pathway for us to follow this day.
Long before there was a Martin or Malcolm X,
there was a Douglas or Garvey.
Medgar Evers was shot dead;
he walked the road to help carry us to this point.
Soldiers of the railroad, colorless, have sheltered many in their care.

Our ancestors have created a pathway for us to follow this day.
It is a path that has brought us to the White House.
It is history that has bonded all races to elect the president.
A collective minority has become the majority and has elected a president.

Our ancestors have created a pathway for us to follow this day.
President Barack Obama, is the leader in that pathway—he and his family.
You, President Obama, represent everyone in this country proudly.
But you are a part of us, like you were a part of your mother.

Forward

He leaned forward.
There were coal mines deep in the Virginia woods.
He related not to this group who spoke.
Yet the end spoke the truth of victory, Virginia victory.

He leaned forward.
The goal was to finish undone tasks that lay before his eyes.
The stumbling blocks were piled high with bricks of concrete.
With the people's support solid, he sought to continue his path.

He leaned forward.
Many fought him to eliminate the path of forwardness.
He held focus; his goal never strayed.
They labored and fought to destroy the people's choice.

He leaned forward.
Pitfalls came his way.
He never stopped to knitpick, he rode with the people.
His moves always elevated higher, and in the end,
he won by a ton with voters.

Monologue Binders

What, an empty-chair monologue, filled with a binder of women?
An old man stood over a chair and did a monologue with
his wandering mind.
He appeared to be out of place while Romney smiled.
Romney was a misfit until President Obama went to sleep
in his first debate.

What, an empty-chair monologue, full of a binder of women?
Overnight, Romney sprang forward just to die a slow death later.
He brought forth untruths, and it didn't matter for a short time.
When the jeep beep went to China, people cried out, "Enough is enough."

What, an empty-chair monologue, full of a binder of women?
Women gathered and cried out, "We are not binders!"
Look around; we stand in each field that has embraced you.
Our spirits are in the cracks of every corner.

What, an empty-chair monologue, full of a binder of women?
We bind, but we are not binders, deny us not, engage us into all areas.
Monologue, not air, brings forth those who have sung and paid the price.
Fill the chair with tomorrow's miles of smiles, not days of gloom.

Brazenly False

Brazenly false, President Obama has outsourced Jeeps to China.
Are we the people without a brain?
It's a Karl Rove reality.
Stop; think. We, the people, occasionally put our minds to work.

Brazenly false, President Obama has outsourced Jeeps to China.
Let's get the groove in the move to speak the truth on his level.
Paul Ryan's budget is not the one I will honor once president.
Social Security will not be privatized; I have my own plans.

Brazenly false, President Obama has outsourced Jeeps to China.
The president said Benghazi was not terror related.
We are not trying to suppress votes.
We are trying to eliminate fraudulent voting.

Brazenly false, President Obama has outsourced Jeeps to China.
Seven hours standing in line to cast one's vote.
Suppress not me; I will go forth with all power to vote.
False truth brought not victory; it was the game of honor.

III

Workaholic

Brawl

Who won without a fighter's lick when they brawled?
He slept through the first debate.
I yelled, "I put my head down and cried without a tear."
I tried desperately to debate your policies through the TV to no avail.

Who won without a fighter's lick when they brawled?
He approached to shout, and an untruth rang out.
I felt the pain of many, and we all cried out.
We knew the words that pealed from Romney's lips were not real or true.

Who won without a fighter's lick when they brawled?
You stepped up with fame in your name.
An untruth trail you stopped, stamped and sealed—gone was it.
Like a teacher grading a paper, mistakes corrected, untruth revealed.

Who won without a fighter's lick when they brawled?
It wasn't a brawl.
It was a knockout to continue your policies.
It was a clear direction to move forward, not backward.

Battleground

Battleground states he claimed.
It was fierce.
Yet he prevailed.
He yielded not a word to reveal his strategy.

Battleground states he claimed.
Not an eye did he blink.
Steal his links they tried; button-tight security, it was not to be.
Not a ground to be found uncovered, they were the wolves
with cotton feet.

Battleground states he claimed.
The opposing team was strong and ruthless.
He held ground, stood tall with his team altogether,
and brought in the win.
Early that night, they bound that win with a beautiful bow.

Battleground states he claimed.
Trump posted, "To the street we will go to deny the electoral victory!"
Quicker than a mouse, Trump unposted it, popular votes,
there he claimed too.
Who is this President Barack Hussein Obama?

The Ghostly Past

Two years had passed; a new beginning had begun.
A two-year ghost vanished.
It's time to banish the debate; he has claimed victory.
He won on his records; now honor his victory.

Two years had passed; a new beginning had begun.
The people say his current position is the only one that matters.
His second term was based upon his current policies.
Now, it's time to allow the people's voices to be represented.

Two years had passed; a new beginning had begun.
Two years gone, policies brought before you, you shelved them all.
Now you cry and say, "Off the cliff we go; back up two years."
The people want real, deep-rooted changes, backward not, forward yes.

Two years had passed; a new beginning had begun.
One-time president, not a reality, he has not fallen in the ditch others
have dug for their fish catch.
The foundation goals have been formulated by the people.
President Obama represents the people; he has chosen their side,
a soldier of the people.

The Disabilities Treaty

The Disabilities Treaty cried out to be signed.
Let those who have little or no respect for the UN sign off, please.
Let America continue to be progressive.
Amendment in the Treaty says you cannot go into an American
court to sue.

The Disabilities Treaty cried out to be signed.
America has progressive laws for those with disabilities.
Many countries lack this progressive state that America holds.
Why stand with Farris, people of conscience? The helpless are calling out.

The Disabilities Treaty cried out to be signed.
UN travels far and near and sees all.
It is through those without a voice UN seeks out to help.
You escape not your box to serve those without a voice to cast
the right vote.

The Disabilities Treaty cried out to be signed.
Men with conscience serve people and not their boxed-up fear.
The president has served those well with disabilities.
He reinstated an executive order to hire
additional federal employees with disabilities.

The Disabilities Treaty cried out to be signed.
The UN seeks to serve all, not a boxed few.
Out of fear, many people put themselves into a cage.
They encage it themselves on an island bolted with a steel lock.

Workaholic

He's a workaholic for you, me, and all.
The future rides on his Energy Partnership for Americans.
He's a workaholic for you, me, and all.
He fully funded Veterans Administration for those who fought
for our freedom.

He's a workaholic for you, me, and all.
He reinstated an executive order to hire numerous persons with disabilities.
He's a workaholic for you, me, and all.
He moved to carry out the Moscow Treaty to reduce nuclear forces.

He's a workaholic for you, me, and all.
He provided mortgage modifications for those who were losing their homes.
He's a workaholic for you, me, and all.
He's freed all to work in the military without threats over their heads.

He's a workaholic for you, me, and all.
He opens his mind to listen to the people and respond appropriately.
He's a workaholic for you, me, and all.
He moves us constantly always forward.

Leaning Forward

He has moved forward each step he has taken.
He has proved to be a peacemaker who received the Nobel Peace Prize.
He marches to the drum of Dr. Martin Luther King Jr.
He's a devoted family man; he's a model husband and father.

He has moved forward each step he has taken.
It was he who understood the impact of women
who are heads of households.
It was the Lilly Ledbetter Law that opened fair pay for women.
It is he who believed violence against women should be eradicated.

He has moved forward each step he has taken.
Children can now receive the care they need to stay healthy.
The Universal Health Bill lingers not; it has come to be a reality.
Preexisting conditions are guarded not by insurance companies.

He has moved forward each step he has taken.
Recession has been put on hold; employment rate is on the move.
The war has ended in Iraq, and Osama Bin Laden has returned to dust.
He fights vigorously for the will of the middle class.

Recovery Steps

The road to recovery has put a load on your shoulders.
You have been given a second chance to meet the challenges.
Challenges have been placed upon your watch from another administration.
You have handled the challenges well.

The road to recovery has put a load on your shoulder.
You kept the bell from ringing into recession.
You brought this country out of a mold that was about to fold.
You sought to latch on to our needs to march us forward.

The road to recovery has put a load on your shoulder.
Many thought the recovery has been too much like a toad.
But reality says, "We are not losing jobs at this point."
Initially, the continued loss of jobs was a major factor when you took office.

The road to recovery has put a load on your shoulder.
You have sought to implement policies that are helpful to the economy.
Unfortunately, the House of Representatives was not supportive.
You have continued to move forward in spite of this lack of support.

Rice

A price will not be paid for the bizarre attack on Rice.
The State Department, Pentagon, and CIA are charged with protection.
The Republicans attacked Rice personally, not these agencies.
Rice is a Rhodes Scholar and a seasoned policy maker.

A price will not be paid for the bizarre attack on Rice.
They stalked her portentous nomination.
They alleged this Rhodes Scholar stands as an incompetent person.
Let it be said, I'm angry because I am.

A price will not be paid for the bizarre attack on Rice.
Like a mouse, the House jumped in with numerous signatures.
They sought the duty of the Senate before it was a nomination.
She delivered talking points from the intelligence community, misled not.

A price will not be paid for the bizarre attack on Rice.
An intelligence community provided her with coded speaking information.
Rice did not personalize received information.
They willfully and deliberately sought to taint her on levels undeserved.

A price will not be paid for the bizarre attack on Rice.
She withdrew to mute mouths so America can progressively move forward.
She had not any involvement with Benghazi attack; she withdrew. Now what?
American security failed in Benghazi, not at her feet, a terrorist attack.

A price will not be paid for the bizarre attack on Rice.
Rice was requested to speak, short of Clinton unable to go forward.
The McCain Bunch wanted President Obama for a White House conspiracy.
They have not and will not be able to develop evidence of a true cover-up.

A price will not be paid for the bizarre attack on Rice.
Rice stood above all and she made a classic withdrawal.
They had the audacity to try to use her against the president?
Or maybe it was a target of race, so goes the signatories with white males.

IV

The People Spoke

Concede

The votes are coming in, and I'm anxious as a hound dog, looking for his prey.
It appears the president may lose, but I'm still hopeful.
I am sitting on edge, waiting and hoping; this nation needs his leadership.
Will President Obama remain in office?

The votes are coming in, and I'm anxious as a hound dog, looking for his prey.
Without shoes to track him, the governor may slip into office.
His deceptions may steal the president's ability
to take the country forward.
We, the people, the country, the world, will lose if that should come.

The votes are coming in, and I'm anxious as a hound dog, looking for his prey.
The hours are getting longer and longer, and the eyes are weaker.
The race is moving two by two, closer and closer.
The hound dog is howling at the door, calling out for his prey.

The votes are coming in, and I'm anxious as a hound dog, looking for his prey.
The crowd just went into jubilation; the president has the Electoral votes.
The governor's pathway to victory had just been completely cut off,
yet he's not ready to concede.
The governor, not ready to concede,
is typical with how he has run his campaign.

Voters have come and cast their choices; the calm sea has come upon me.
We will now continue the pathway of forwardness with President Obama.
His standards have remained high; he has not wallowed or swallowed in
the dirt that was laid in his roadway
Finally, the governor comes to the stage, looking like a zombie, to concede.

Minority Becomes Majority

When did the minority become the majority?
The day President Obama became a two-term president.
The day Asians said, "You lack nothing with us. We have your back and front.
You are universal. You break not your word. You speak with great volume."

When did the minority become the majority?
The day women cast their votes to represent themselves.
He had their families in his care.
The real meal was at their hands; family will receive an equal weekly check.

When did the minority become the majority?
The day the youth said, "Our brighter future will come through you."
Education is the key; you have already opened doors to make it real.
Today's time will be history that comes tomorrow.

When did the minority become the majority?
Though smaller in numbers, white males also made an impact.
Umbrella eyes opened up to shed anew from the old.
To step out from the old, it must be a wedded thought to move forward.

When did the minority become the majority?
The day Hispanics stepped into tomorrow and not yesterday.
Cuba was a distant yesterday; immigration became the manhole of today.
It was the day they viewed their current condition before casting their votes.

When did the minority become the majority?
Clarence Thomas, a Supreme Court Justice, represents the Republican Party.
Romney switched repeatedly like a fantasy witch swings on a broom.
Romney's unclear policy, inconsistency, with his party voter suppression
attempt, sent blacks to the poll in great numbers.

When did the minority become the majority?
The day people voted to represent the humanness of man, not race.
The day people looked into another's heart and saw the pounding of self.
The day people looked beyond color to embrace another human being.

River of Hope

Our president still has a river of hope.
He walks with light shoes, with a heavy load on his back.
How is he able to strut in such a way and carry the world on his back?
He moves with such grace in the midst of confusion, abroad and home.

Our president still has a river of hope.
They stick him with thorns and needles; he doesn't bend.
Task oriented, he stands firmly, cooperative if you wish.
He still moves forward with an olive branch
if you choose to join the people's mission.

Our president still has a river of hope.
He is strong, yet he's able to generate his inner feelings for you to feel.
The mass looked beyond those who scandalized his name, for him to lead.
He is older and wiser; perhaps that is why he is more hopeful now than ever.

Our president still has a river of hope.
There was nothing left unsaid about this president.
He moves forward without a stumble, and he heeds not to destructibility.
He is President Obama, a two-term president, with a river of hope.

Today's Hope

He was rebuffed, doors slammed in his face. Still he stood strong.
The road was hard, the journey long; he picked himself up and fought back.
Let them now come together; crushed they have been. Let's rebuild again.
He still listens willingly with an olive branch across the hall.

He was rebuffed, doors slammed in his face. Still he stood strong.
He sought bipartisanship to no avail. Will it finally come now?
The Electoral and Popular votes stamped him; the people have spoken.
The people stood against walls and halls in great numbers to usher him in.

He was rebuffed, doors slammed in his face. Still he stood strong.
Let this election speak to those who have marked his prior years.
They called him Un-American, a noncitizen, and a gorilla.
The people have cried out for them to build a bridge across the canal.

He was rebuffed, doors slammed in his face. Still he stood strong.
In spite of these hardships, he believes strongly in this nation's future.
He is more hopeful today than yesterday.
It is this country's freedom that allows such differences of opinions.

He was rebuffed, doors slammed in his face. Still he stood strong.
The House Speaker, on election night.
chose to go to bed rather than speak to the President.
He honored not this, but he acknowledged the Speaker's will to choose.
Yet he said, "I am more hopeful today than yesterday."

Romney

He walked on stage like a zombie.
He spoke briefly to the occasion.
His concession speech was short and to the point.
He came forward two hours later with his concession speech.

He walked on stage like a zombie.
He walked on stage alone like a lost child, searching for the unknown.
He proceeded to speak; he appeared to be shell-shocked.
Was he shell-shocked?

He walked on stage like a zombie.
President Obama had won with a minority as a majority.
His blank face read, "You mean whites did not put me into office?"
No! Asians, Hispanics, blacks, women, youth,
and some white males voted as a block for the best man!
It was as if he had been living in a bubble, free from reality.

He walked on stage like a zombie.
It was a pitiful sight to see,
but I was still strong for Obama, the President.
Two hours later, he came to give a concession speech
when the election was obviously over hours earlier.
Perhaps it took Romney two hours to get his composure;
but the country now
had to proceed in an orderly manner with the
two-term president elect, President Obama.

His Stand

It was his last hurrah, electoral stand, but not his last stand.
His electoral results proved he is the real deal for the people.
The popular votes curved him into a landmark.
Does he stand as a fluke, first? No.

It was his last hurrah, electoral stand, but not his last stand.
Shoulders extended, tone of voice firm, Rice echoed information received.
Face and lace me with your allegations.
That is not a pot to boil, McCain, stop it,
torture not an innocent reputation.

It was his last hurrah, electoral stand, but not his last stand.
Echoing steps of another, Graham, you are not a man of the people.
How can you be an affirmation of the people,
seeking to destroy the innocent?
You must move and groove with facts, free yourself of emotions.

It was his last hurrah, electoral stand, but not his last stand.
Oppose me if you wish; you have just received an electoral wipeout.
Pack up your emotions, bury your loses, and move to serve the people.
We are duty bound, two dichotomies, the people have chosen the one.

The Mess

The mess keeps on coming.
It's over, move on, and stop being stagnated.
He has won; the people rule, step back and out.
Four years back now, McCain still accepts not the main course.

The mess keeps on coming.
The people have chosen wisely.
You lost because people elected another to lead.
It's painful and hard, that's a part of reality, now skip away.

The mess keeps on coming.
This road has locked you out and about.
A new day has dawned, not for you, but for him.
He continues to lead.

The mess keeps on coming.
He carries the country's load well.
The others ring their bells together like a pack of wolves.
Progressively, you must gather to accept the new, not to hinder it.

The McCain Bunch

Politically, you have lost; now you are out to destroy.
She stands firmly.
Is it the color of chocolate?
Are you able to move ahead to release your inner prejudice?

Politically, you have lost; now you are out to destroy.
She provided information that was authorized, yet you have her marked.
You have tried for years to politically harm
the president through his cabinet.
Why not concern yourself with security, not Rice?

Politically, you have lost; now you are out to destroy.
The price you hope to post on Rice's head will not succeed.
You should develop strategies to prevent death's duplication.
We mourn the loss of those who have gone; politicize it not.

Politically, you have lost; now you are out to destroy.
You have been on his attack since you lost previously, four years
back; it's time to let go.
Prime time is not yours; the president is the head man, the Big Boss.
A man above you and all, with organizational skills and
top-rated, take a chill pill.

Obsession with Succession

Speaker One:	Personally, I can't believe they voted for Obama over Governor Romney.
Speaker Two:	What do you mean?
	Why are you calling him Governor and the President by his first name?
	He is the President of the USA; he represents everyone in this country.
	Romney was a one-time state Governor of Massachusetts.
	The President was reelected to serve the people, and that includes you.
Speaker One:	No. He is not my President. I am going to secede from this country.
Speaker Two:	Hey! What? You are going to do what? How are you going to do that?
Speaker One:	We are going to sign a petition and submit it to Washington.
Speaker Two:	We? Who is going to sign a petition?
Speaker One:	The people he doesn't represent.
Speaker Two:	He represents you whether you cast him your vote or not. He is the winner.
	He won the popular votes with the Electoral College Votes.
	It is he who stands the highest within the USA, and that is the greatest truth.
	Recognize it, acknowledge it, accept it, and let's move to work together.
Speaker One:	Never will I accept the lazy food stamp President!
Speaker Two:	OMG, please guide my tongue; signing a petition may not be beneficial.
	It is practically impossible for any state to secede from the USA?
	How would you economically, militarily, and medically assist the voters?

The People's Mark

He has the mark of a genius, implanted with exposure.
Did he not implant the word *hope* in the hopeless?
What happened with the fluke?
You claimed his first win was a fluke; he won a second term.

He has the mark of a genius, implanted with exposure.
People voted for a change rolled into the word *hope*.
He carried his father's dream for a better world.
His father influenced his life, although present he was not.

He has the mark of a genius, implanted with exposure.
He had an absent father who was favorably viewed.
Positive male images surrounded roles he undertook.
Father images he sought, echoing through his grandfather
and other role models.

He has the mark of a genius, implanted with exposure.
Through shared letters, a better understanding arose with his father.
He embraced his ideas to motivate him to great heights.
He understood: his grandfather, the cook's world view, versus Wall Street.

He has the mark of a genius, implanted with exposure.
He carried his father's dream for a better world.
He championed a second term to continue the choice of the people.
He is not only the choice of the people, he is an element of the people.

V

Second Term

The Journey

His enchanted journey has taken him to the White House.
He was a boy who lived without his father's presence.
His mother rooted him with worldly knowledge.
He walked hand in hand with his grandfather.

His enchanted journey has taken him to the White House.
He observed those who came within his presence.
He lived to experience some childhood negative name-calling.
He overcame other faults because he was possessed with love.

His enchanted journey has taken him to the White House.
Educationally, he traveled far and near to mark one road his father took.
He buried himself in community advocacies.
He chose the love of his life; they wed and two children emerged.

His enchanted journey has taken him to the White House.
Capitol Hill he served first; it was a road to the White House.
He embraced the belief while few believed it was an obtainable goal.
Until one day, it became a reality, and they all said it was a fluke.

His enchanted journey has taken him twice to the White House.
His win, the second time was greater than the first.
It left all in a pickle with the suppressed vote attempt.
His hair is a little grayer, but he still has that swagger strut.
With that swagger stride he stepped in the White House,
for the second time.

Benghazi

It was sad a day when we lost four American lives.
It was a deadly attack on people who have served the world of man.
It took Ambassador Stevens's life with three others.
A crowd's riot was used to escalate this act of violence.

It was a sad day when we lost four American lives.
President Obama, was somber when he spoke to the nation.
There weren't any political points to be made with either party.
Unfortunately, some wanted to sing "faulthood"; we were not bound as one.

It was a sad day when we lost four American lives.
The president's heart was felt when he spoke of his deep sorrow.
Osama Bin Laden walks not through his reign.
It is through those soft shoes that evildoers fall hard;
their payday will come.

It was a sad day when we lost four American lives.
It was a protest that had spun out of control.
It may have been a protest with more than one agenda.
In the end, four lay dead; we should be of one accord, not a thousand in one.

It was a sad day when we lost Ambassador Stevens's life with three others.

Vexed

Vexed with his reelection, they support him not.
It has angered opposition.
They have chosen not to budge an inch on taxes with the wealthy.
They seem not to care about his popular and electoral wins.

Vexed with his reelection, they support him not.
It has angered opposition.
The president has yielded to compromise on an item, but they respond not.
Medicare, they demand an age upward; the elderly cry, "Not an inch upward."

Vexed with his reelection, they support him not.
It has angered opposition.
It is with those who have worked lifelong years since childhood.
The knees are weak and the legs squeaky like cracks on the floor.

Vexed with his reelection, they support him not.
It has angered opposition.
They seek not cost of living with Medicare.
They seek qualifications to be edged up two years.

Vexed with his reelection, they support him not.
It has angered opposition.
It is through seniors the GOP wishes to cut funds, and leave the wealthy.
The popular voters spoke for their cause when they sent Romney packing.

Vexed with his reelection, they support him not.
It has angered opposition.
President Obama has saddled himself with a solution left upon his shoulders.
Many are tired of self-motivation goals, escaping the needs of the people.

Second Term

Many thought President Obama would only serve one term.
The day he was reelected, reality became a fact.
Unable to cope, many took a chill pill and went to bed without a word.
It was reality wrapped up, and sealed with the popular and electoral votes.

Many thought President Obama would only serve one term.
The failure to complete a deficit reduction last year was now
in their hands.
Their hope did not become a reality; the president was reelected
Now their failure to act last year, was now back to the front.

Many thought President Obama would only serve one term,
Congress wanted to act with a new president—hopefully, Romney,
not the current one.
They did not want to stop the expiration of Bush-era tax cuts.
We had hoped this will be put to rest before the new Congress convenes.

Many thought President Obama would only serve one term.
He has served one; now he is serving two.
Neither the goal nor the President changed;
the need is to act now, this day.
Let Congress negotiate without jeopardizing the middle class or the needy.

The Man of the Year

He represents the new America; extended lines of voters said it all.
Imperfect he is, but a perfect *Time*'s choice for the **Person of the Year**
They had mocked President Obama as a fluke.
They called him a hopeless stuff of nothing that sought useless change.

He represents the new America; extended lines of voters said it all.
He is measured by his accomplishments; America is recession-free.
His reelection said it all, not an ephemeral many sought to make it.
He implemented changes in the insurance system with a tax cut extension.

He represents the new America; extended lines of voters said it all.
He saved General Motors, deregulated and restructured failing agencies.
Uniform service gay members walk not in closets with their partners.
He stopped wars and avoided new ones.

He represents the new America; extended lines of voters said it all.
History will disappoint those who called his presidency a fluke.
He created new ways campaigns are run.
He has set a new tone for all to follow, an honest one of strength.

VI

Newtown

Assault Weapons

An assault weapon at home, for what?
One that shoots thirty rounds within a second.
Military style, what was on her mind when it was purchased?
It blazed through a locked door, shattered it into pieces,
to reach the innocent.

An assault weapon at home, for what?
A handicapped child practices at a gun range with backup violent videos.
Blame the parent, the weapon, videos, and the mental deficiency carrier.
Until this is collectively dealt with, unfortunately, this may come again.

An assault weapon at home, for what?
The mentally deficient person needs to be nervous appropriately.
Parents sometime impose their expectations on their challenged children.
People with mental illness should receive medical care and not lockups.

An assault weapon at home, for what?
Who can say, perhaps society has failed both mother and son?
Jail should not be forced upon a mentally ill person who needs assistance.
A person should guard and oversee activities of the mentally ill at all times.

An assault weapon at home, for what?
War weapons are for war, a home should be free of any war weapons.
Things have to be done, but what and when, Mr. President?
How can we embrace now and allow things to remain the same?

Dad

It was the dad who came, not the President.
He came to help us surrender into a form of peace, not to forget.
He came with a heavy heart, bleeding for all who stood with the lost.
Hearts of nation he carried, but he stood there bleeding
as a parent that day.

It was the dad who came, not the President.
He hugged and held us dearly that day, one by one.
What a burden he carried, embracing each family separately.
President Obama's pain echoed through a parent's loss, a tear wiped.

It was the dad who came, not the President.
He came with heavily ladened shoulders—
Shoulders that spoke for a nation, a heart that stood as a parent.
We were honored, but back it goes for just another moment with my child.

It was the dad who came, not the President.
A mentally ill person with an assault weapon had stolen lives of children.
Let the laws be free to serve the mentally ill, not to cage them first.
Let us seek to curve this madness that repeats itself much too often.

The Visitor

I

The President came to town.
We are still in deep sorrow, but his presence told us the nation mourns too.
I lost my angel who had a voice like an angel in heaven.
It is a voice that I will long to hear, yet the stillness of sound will remain.

The President came to town.
After many days had gone,
my world could not conceive of her not returning home.
An unbelievable reality shocked my world that day.
I sought to turn the clock back, but the clock had been broken.

The President came to town.
Words have been spoken, tears have been shared, hearts are broken still.
It meant the world to sit with you, Mr. President.
Yet, I would zap it away, if I could have another moment with my child.

The President came to town.
Thank you, President Obama, for coming to town to share our greatest loss.
Is there a recovery road to this great madness?
Not for me, I lost a wonderful, innocent, joyful life that's not replaceable.

The President came to town.
Mr. President, we look to you for our children to have not died in vain.
Tragedy continues to fall upon the lives of our children.
We cry, we mourn, and our children's lives continue to be lost repeatedly.

The President came to town.
We were somber then and now; it is our children we hold close in our heart.
It is now time for the slaughtering of our children to stop, Mr. President.
What will and can we do, Mr. President?

B

Tragedies

How can we end these tragedies?
They keep repeating themselves.
We have hurt, and anger is all about.
We are somber in mood.

How can we end these tragedies?
The pain and hurt are too deep to bear without care for change.
Will families drift slowly apart as they come together as one in the nation?
Families and nation come together as one, but will they slowly drift apart?
Alter these acts of violence through movies, gun control,
or mental health issues.

How can we end these tragedies?
Will Sandy Hook be the turning point to roll the ball forward?
Let it be so; children of innocence must not be slaughtered.
The four lost lives in Alabama changed Civil Rights; let this be so too.

How can we end these tragedies?
Commitments on both sides must walk forward hand in hand.
Let us not lose the hurt and anger we both have
before changes take their place.
We are not powerless to move; we must safeguard our children, the future.

Too Many

Three plus none—mental health, gun control, and violent games—stand we.
The man lingers on the street or home cuddled up with a mind uncontrolled.
Lunatics with guns touch the trigger repeatedly in alternated years.
Guns, the most dangerous game of violence, let's make gun control a reality.

Three plus none—mental health, gun control, and violent games—stand we.
Thirty bullets fired less than a second, military-style gun, home ownership.
What was the state of her mind when she purchased such firepower?
Guns, guns out of control, thirteen mass shootings this year look in our faces.

Three plus none—mental health, gun control, and violent games—stand we.
Today my mind runs rapidly; I struggle from corner to corner.
Night and day have come into one, and I have order not.
Home I live, reality not here; my parents hide me in the corner.

Three plus none—mental health, gun control, and violent games—stand we.
The newest game has arrived, the most deadly.
Will it desensitize me, not to feel pain?
Will I go out to play this game with humans today that my ears are plugged into?

Three plus none—mental health, gun control, and violent games—stand we.
This nation is in a state of anguish, filled with deep sorrow.
There are tears we cry, none stop.
When tears are there, we try to function, but we are in a zombie state.

Three plus none—mental health, gun control, and violent games—stand we.
This time, this should not go away, twenty innocent children died.
Two previous presidents, Bush and Clinton, have stood before the nation.
The nation stood with them in times of deep sorrow, repetition has come again.

Three plus none—mental health, gun control, and violent games—stand we.
President Obama, we stand with you. Our hearts are broken too, speak to change.
Tears are all around us; we cry inward and out. The nation shares the pain.
Mr. President, the nation stands with you, move us forward.

Killer Weapons

Guns are weapons that kill.
Assault weapons have industrial strength.
They have been created to slaughter by the dozens.
They were not created to kill a gang or deer in the forest.

Guns are weapons that kill.
Mr. President, you are the one that can curtail these shootings.
Gun violence takes thousands of lives a year, alter this, Mr. President.
You have accomplished many goals since you have become president.

Guns are weapons that kill.
We look for you to bring a solution to the madness that
echoes the guns—
The guns that take lives day by day; we weep to ease the pain we carry.
They say bring more guns to stop the killings.

Guns are weapons that kill.
College students armed with guns; slaughter continues still, none stop.
Now, bring guns into little ones' school? I think not.
Let ideas run free, surrounded not with gun power ready to explode.

Weapons without a Cause

They are weapons without a cause, other than to slaughter.
It can be less than a minute, not one, but sixty can be dead as lead.
Break and enter, not needed, buckshot shotgun, sufficient.
It's not a dozen-egg game, it's children, innocent ones,
dying without a cause.

They are weapons without a cause, other than to slaughter.
Guns in the hands of crazy people, worst than the Wild West.
Emotional killings, territory gang fighting, it is the taker of innocent lives.
One by one, two by two, or those that fall in dozens,
they all breathe no more.

They are weapons without a cause, other than to slaughter.
The ill cry out, and we take no notice.
They rumble in mansions too, as homeless ones rumble in trash piles.
We cannot stand innocently, free from it all; we must have them
make changes.

They are weapons without a cause, other than to slaughter.
A man, an evil man, an ill man, came to exercise a right to own a gun.
With this ownership, he killed innocent lives.
We stand, we mourn, we cry, and the killings keep on;
it's time the killings stop.

Hadiya

She lay dead as so many others did from gang violence.
When will it stop, now or never?
Guns are all around us, increasing rapidly in this environment.
Children die day and night; the sound of the bullet keeps on popping.

She lay dead as so many others did from gang violence.
She played while others danced on Inaugural Day, near the White House.
Days later she lay dead; her voice was silenced by a bullet.
A beautiful, innocent voice has been stolen.

She lay dead as so many others did from gang violence.
Her funeral came with a packed audience to mourn her fate.
She stepped into the realm of the White House on one glorious day,
days later she was in a morgue.
Her innocent carefree walk would be no more in this world of violence.

She lay dead as so many others did from gang violence
The park shielded her from the rain, but not the popping of the gun.
The tree was her umbrella on that rainy day.
She was gone faster than the blinking of an eye.

She lay dead as so many others did from gang violence.
The First Lady came to bid her farewell.
The First Lady also cried for those who have yonder gone.
Hadiya, we pray this madness will one day come to an end.

VII

Fiscal Cliff

Make The Deal

Congress, will you make the budget deal?
We, the people, appeal to you.
Search your soul and make a deal.
The fiscal cliff we do not want to reach.

Congress, will you make the budget deal?
In a dungeon now you stand; do not risk another political backlash.
Political we take not a stand.
It's the survival mode of the middle class.

Congress, will you make the budget deal?
Let it be not another day that we are forced
to embrace an economic crises.
President Obama has repeatedly extended his hand.
Catch his hand and move forward to avoid the recession.

Congress, will you make the budget deal?
The middle class is standing now on a banana-pile, rocky-edged mountain.
Unless you make the deal, we will be compelled to drift into another lane.
Sweep us not away, care to avoid a curved crooked lane and make a deal.

Averted Plan B

They stood with the door wide open, ran, and headed for the cliff.
Boehner's Plan B sought to avert help to the middle class—
A plan that extended tax cuts set to expire at a year's end.
Tax rates, increased one million over he sought, Boehner's Plan denied.

They stood with the door wide open, ran, and headed for the cliff.
Supporting not President Obama's Plan,
Boehner substituted his Plan B.
What, he couldn't get his party to support his nonnegotiable plan B?
Many opposed Plan B; signals had tripled, wrapped the poll with notes.

They stood with the door wide open, ran, and headed for the cliff.
The president continued to work to avert the fiscal cliff.
Holidays were here, and tax rates above $250,000 stood
without an answer.
Republicans said, "Raise not taxes," while the Democrats said,
"Yes to taxes."

They stood with the door wide open, ran, and headed for the cliff.
Bipartisan solution must come quickly to avert the fiscal cliff.
It must come to protect the middle class and our economic system.
The fiscal cliff is hanging on the edge with one foot on a banana pile.

Unsettled Holidays

The holidays are few and coming.
The children will be soon holiday breaking.
Michelle and I hope the fiscal cliff will be soon settled.
The middle class must be sitting on the edge, waiting to receive a release.

The holidays are few and coming.
There are Presidential Challenges nonstop.
This is one I had hoped would be arrested in days yonder gone.
It goes deep; let me try to arrest this call, which is the cry, of the people.

The holidays are few and coming.
Congress is now standing on 2 percent.
It doesn't want the rich to pay additional taxes, the 2 percent.
Let's relieve the middle class, square responsibility across the board.

The holidays are few and coming.
We are days short from the cliff drop.
Maybe the people's gift will be the fiscal cliff gone, arrested.
I must deal with the challenges standing before me.
The holidays are few and coming.

Unify

Let the President propose his plans while the Congress disposes of them.
The Tea Baggers' power appeared to have been a fluke.
The President has been reelected, don't whine and cry, yours was rejected.
Let's work together to create a better society.

Let the President propose his plans while the Congress disposes of them.
Unity is a challenge both for the Democrats and the Republicans.
Let the government avoid a useless stalemate emphasizing party only.
Save the people who are nearing a fiscal cliff; let them survive another day.

Let the President propose his plans while the Congress disposes of them.
The majority of the Electoral College has clearly,
victoriously chosen President Obama.
Lick your wounds, let there be no sour grapes; the winner has been chosen.
It's time to accept reality and move to work for this country.

Let the President propose his plan while the Congress disposes of them.
Get in line to help implement plans to enhance the lives of the people.
Without the President's plans, this country will go into a downward spiral.
Take the red, blue, and the two parties out; let's move to unify the country.

Partisan Bickering

Partisan Bickering has overridden the needs of the people.
Why should the rich be taxed when they trickle money down to the needy?
Hey, let me run to catch that patch of trickling-down money.
I'm only part of the middle class, hanging by a thread; the poor are
knocking at my door.

Partisan Bickering has overridden the needs of the people.
Please take some taxes off my shoulders, for the middle class I stand.
Hey, less than 1 percent of the rich's taxes supersede my entire income.
You cry, "I die, medicine and food gone yonder."

Partisan Bickering has overridden the needs of the people.
Mystify me not; I am furious, you rebel against more taxes on the rich.
Which is it, more daily struggle on me or tax on the rich?
The wealthy are lined with riches, the middle class fighting
to stay above water.

Partisan Bickering has overridden the needs of the people.
Taxes are a reality we must all cope with in America.
The middle class has always fought their battle well.
Their pockets rattle less than the rich, so let the rich share the taxes.

Deadline

The deadline looms; will we drown or swim?
The cliffhanger hangs all around this ground.
The holidays are approaching, and still I stand without a job.
Where is the cry that will save my bare existence?

The deadline looms, will we drown or swim?
I have worked hard for years.
Now, I am overly taxed and you let the rich escape?
What fairness lies within that arena?

The deadline looms; will we drown or swim?
Pension is short to none, tax that out, homeless I'll be.
There's not a trickle down here; tax on them too, and let me breathe.
Which yoyo game they play this day? What, will I have, food or medicines?

The deadline looms; will we drown or swim?
It's a hostage situation, hanging on the edge. Where is the care?
Recession, do you dare not vote to end this stalemate?
The rush is about to push the bush over the cliff; the end is edging closer.

Protection of Armor

Protect the President, Father.
There are those with wretched souls who wish him mighty harm.
Let your armor surround him constantly.
Let your greatness come upon him every second.

Protect the President, Father.
Let your light always be within his shadow.
Father, let him stand within your grace, filled with your compassion.
Let your mighty mercy never leave his side.

Protect the President, Father.
Let your love shower him always with your mercy.
Let your guidance remain with him when foes come within his presence.
Let him continue to have hope, for the weak and the vulnerable.

Protect the President, Father.
He believes this country will move forward with great courage.
He has renewed hope although racism still remains a factor.
A coalition of the minority has created a majority to
stamp him as President.
Father, will you keep your armor of protection over this President?

Fiscal Cliff

The cliff is steep and the valley is deep.
Antitax pledge runs high with one unit.
"Deal not if the rich ring free," says he.
Taxes must come, and the rich must pay their way.

The cliff is steep and the valley is deep.
Fear is near, and the fever must break.
Trickling down, the wealth has escaped the needy.
The top must pay and not escape another day.

The cliff is steep and the valley is deep.
The overloaded middle is sinking by the barrels.
The cry is loud; who will hear?
The wealthy ears are locked.

The cliff is steep and the valley is deep.
Who will come to level the odds?
The people are filled with aches and pains.
Is the president our only warrior to grant us relief?

Gridlock Temporary Ends

Washington has been synonymous with *gridlock*.
Everything has been latched and pitched and thrown into a ditch.
People stood on edge, hoping for a break.
Imperfect or not, the two parties fought to create a solution.

Washington has been synonymous with *gridlock*.
At the eleventh hour, the Senate Floor rose to the occasion.
A bill was finally passed; the voice of the people was heard.
One step of two achieved, the House waited in the wing to answer.

Washington has been synonymous with *gridlock*.
A climax showdown with the House must come to avert a fiscal cliff.
People waited anxiously for the House to pass
the legislation of the 112th Congress.
Will the House deny this achievable goal?
Will Congress avert the fiscal cliff?

Washington has been synonymous with *gridlock*.
Will the struggling middle class families come to pass?
Despite political threats of noncompromise, the President fought on.
In the end, through President Obama and the skillfulness of Vice President
Joe Biden, the fiscal cliff ends.

Vulnerable or Misfortunate

The vulnerable and the misfortunate are a part of this nation.
The government must and will play a role to help alleviate
poverty among us.
Yet, their plight cannot be relinquished entirely upon the government.
Private enterprise must play an equal role to help alleviate
poverty and unemployment.

The vulnerable and the misfortunate are a part of this nation.
Those in need must never succumb to their position.
When capable, their mind and body must always be open
to alter their lives.
Combine actions, if necessary, must be put into a roller coaster to help
move the unemployed forward with great force when the call comes.

The vulnerable and the misfortunate are a part of this nation.
This nation was built upon hard work and personal sacrifice.
With changing times, responsibility demands bipartisanship.
The nation, private enterprise and individuals must move as one body.

The vulnerable and the misfortunate are a part of this nation.
Together we must move collectively, as one nation and one people.
Changes stand before our eyes in education and apprenticeship.
Let's not play the blame game; it is through bipartisanship change
should and will occur.

Nothing to Cut

Father: Family, we must go into sequestering.
Son: Sequestering! What, what is that?
        I mean, what does that mean?
Father: It is the government's permission to cut spending with you.
Son: Cut spending, what money do we have to cut?
        You have got to have money to spend money.
        Dad, we don't have any money.
        How can we cut food?
        We are using the food pantry now each month.
        We use clothes from others to survive in the weather.
        I am sixteen and don't remember when I have ever had anything new.
        I don't complain; I know you and Mom are struggling hard.
Father: "Son, I am trying to say I lost my job this day.
        I don't know whether homelessness is facing this family."

Middle Class

Does America stand for the middle class?
Will it be the middle class prosperity that will
open closed doors to the jobless poor?
America has proved to have great resilience with many untold crises.
We have survived an ending war and a system
that was once almost broken.
Where do you stand?

Does America stand for the middle class?
Do you believe the trickle-down system will save Americans?
The lives of many steps cannot be dictated by a few enriched.
We must step up and save the lives of those who hold America's future.
Where do you stand?

Does America stand for the middle class?
We must seize the moment for all.
We cannot allow a few to dictate their interests
that lie within their boundary.
America was built upon the poorest to have a chance
to succeed against all odds.
Where do you stand?

Does America stand for the middle class?
Once dignity stood on character;
it was not on an element of a packed wallet.
The poor worked hard and succeeded because
an opportunity was opened, not closed.
The bleakest, the poorest, must have an open road to reach the achievable.
Where do you stand?

The Strength of Our Nation

He says our democracy is rooted in the strength of our constitution.
Does that stand true this day?
Are we bound by an idea that was set forth in a declaration?
Was the declaration set forth for all colors of men when it was written?
Did democracy make it possible for a black man to become president?
Oh, was it just a fluke?

He says our democracy is rooted in the strength of our constitution.
Does that stand true this day?
Are we constantly on a journey bridge to create a reality of self meaning?
How can we execute and secure life for another human being?
Is it possible to have life, liberty, and happiness within ourselves?
We fight to maintain the Republic that the patriots fought years yonder gone.

He says our democracy is rooted in the strength of our constitution.
Does that stand true this day?
Are we bound to eradicate all who walk with slave minds?
What do we do with slave minds if America is free of physical slavery?
Where does freedom really come from that we are compelled to execute on earth?
A man once lived in the world of space, but he was bound in a mind cage.

He says our democracy is rooted in the strength of our constitution.
Does that stand true this day?
Who will carry this nation when we are buried in our tombs?
Will the unborn have the educational tools?
Will Lincoln be the only one to keep the survival of a nation?
Did Lincoln see beyond the clouds in order to project America's future?

He says our democracy is rooted in the strength of our constitution.
Does that stand true this day?
This nation will survive through progressive movements, not stagnation.
How can we stand as one nation if we can't get a budget passed?
Does that mean we can only close rank if an outsider comes into interplay?
How can a party and a race be greater than the people one serves?

Accomplishments

The President's Accomplishments road are filled, yet not completed.
Osama bin Laden's road to justice was closed, a distant cry could be heard.
American jobs were saved, auto loan prepaid in full, recession denied.
Volunteer organizers dedicated hours to impact their community.

The President's Accomplishments road are filled, yet not completed.
"Don't Ask, Don't Tell," it ended with the stroke of a pen.
One step closer to world peace, he has put an end to the Iraq war.
He has executed promises that no other did prior.

The President's Accomplishments road are filled, yet not completed.
Women awaken with thoughts of equal job pay.
He is held high with the United Auto Workers, jobs saved.
Koch Brothers and Oil Companies stand not at his side.

The President's Accomplishments road are filled, yet not completed.
Same-sex marriages evolved; it was a mind changer, he stood anew.
Young people fear deportation not; immigration Dreamers smile.
Obamacare was reinforced through the Supreme Court.

The President's Accomplishments road are filled, yet not completed.
The President represents the people's courses.
He had the heart of fifty states; independents stood with the President.
When the final call came, he was the man of the hour, President Obama.

Polarized Politics

There are politicians who despise this President than between
the voters and the people of this country.
This is not about the President; this is about the people of this country,
United States of America.
Call them ignorant, stumpy, dumb or smart, you choose your word,
or maybe they are just glorified want to be actors or actresses.
The President is hitting pure steel, not a wall of plastic,
Washington's Politicians are grave buried.

There are politicians who despise this President than between
the voters and the people of this country.
When he was reelected, they consciously made a decision not to work
with him on any level.
They said his first election was a fluke and they worked four years
strong to hinder his reelection.
The people proved them wrong with his glorified reelection.

There are politicians who despise this President than between
the voters and the people of this country.
They were shell shocked with his reelection, now they have
chosen not to work for the people of America, not the President.
They have chosen not to release funds to implement properly Obamacare.
They have denied the people's needs—they are self motivated and
they have placed politic over policy.

There are politicians who despise this President than between
the voters and the people of this country.
Republicans have politicized this nation and have refused
to give the people a victory;
it's not a President's lost, it's the people's lost.
They are moving on self motivation and they have denied
the people a gun control victory.
Their objective is not to serve the people because
the President is the head of the household.

What comes first, personal politic or a nation?

Merged

I merged into we and we became one.
Voices were heard with this connection.
Through many voices, President Barack Obama,
was reelected to a second term.
An Opposing Team echoed loudly, and stood firmly
not to support the people's choice.

I merged into we and we became one.
The Opposing Team liked the nation leader not.
Without a thought, this Opposing Team agreed not to service
the people of this nation.
One Nation Under God of the United States of America—we should
stand as one body, with likes or dislikes.

I merged into we and we became one.
This Opposing Team has chosen to put politics over policy.
Until we can put our personal life aside and think only of the
United States of America, perhaps the lone wolf will always be in our midst.
America is a nation that's supposed to be built on democracy,
the majority decision should always rule.

I merged into we and we became one.
This Opposing Team seeks to deny the President any major bill approval.
It is not the denial of the President;
it is the people denial that he represents.
This President and the people of United States of America
have merged into one, "The people's Choice.",

Bibliographies

Cillizza, Chris & Aaron Klake. "Parsing President Obama's 2012 Campaign Kickoff" 5 July 2012. Speech Washington Post

Cohen, Tom. "Rocky start to second term raises questions about Obama approach." CNN. 7 March 2013.

en.wikipedia.org/wiki/Detroit_Automobile_Company

en.wikipedia.org/wiki/Underground_Railroad

Obama, Barrack H. Dreams From My Father. New York: Three River Press, 2006.

Obama, Barrack H. The Audacity Of Hope. New York: Three River Press, 2006.

President Campaigns in Vermont and Maine WASHINGTON, DC. Friday, March 30, 2012

Reuters TV; Reuters News; Colin Powell endorses Obama for second term. 25 October, 2012

Reuters.com. 2012 U.S. Presidential Election I Reuters.com

Reuters TV; Reuters News; White House lists two dozen leaders to meet with Obama on deficit; Obama campaign mulls what to do with lauded ground game. November 12, 2012.

State of the Union 2013: President Obama's address to Congress: February 12, 2013

www.dhs.gov

www.hslda.org/about/staff/attorneys/Farris.asp

www.jbs.org

www.lillyledbetter.com

WNW.reuters.com/article/2012/10/25/us-usa-campaign

www.reuters.com/politics/elections-2012

www.skinheadnation.co.uk/sharpskinheads.htm

www.skinheadnation.co.uk/sharpskinheads.htm

Edwards Brothers Malloy
Thorofare, NJ USA
April 18, 2014